D0340420

sales

Brief Lessons and Inspiring Stories

A book to inspire and celebrate
your achievements.

By Jim Williamson

Edited by Dan Zadra
Designed by Kobi Yamada and Steve Potter
Compendium Inc.

DEDICATION

This book is dedicated to the mentors who guided me; the sales managers who challenged me; the clients who trusted me; the students who followed me; the colleagues who teamed with me; the partners who dreamed with me; and to my wife, Maxine, who believed in me.

ACKNOWLEDGEMENTS

The author and editors sincerely appreciate the following people who contributed invaluable assistance, spirit or content to Lessons Learned: John Becvar, Delores Bergstrom, Dick Beselin, Ron Butler, Tom Black, Steve Cheney, Debbie Cottrell, Ron Crawford, Don Daniels, Curt Dickerson, Cris Dippel, Don Dougherty, Ron Fox, David Haines, Elaine Harwell, Denny Holm, Kelly Holm, Cheryl Hungate, Dick Iversen, Gary Jacobson, Eric Jonson, Harry Mandros, Mark Matteson, Bob Moawad, John Moeller, Anna Nerbovig, Pat O'Day, Vince Pfaff, Dennis Schmahl, Janet Scroggs, Jack Sparacio, Dave Sund, Larry Sund, Ron Tarrant, Greg Tiemann, Lee Tillman, Don Williamson, and Dan Zadra.

WITH SPECIAL THANKS TO

Suzanne Hoonan, President, Advantage Learning, without whose creativity and guidance this book would still be merely a good idea.

CREDITS

Edited by Dan Zadra
Designed by Kobi Yamada and Steve Potter

ISBN: 1-888-387-76-9

Printed in Hong Kong

TABLE OF CONTENTS

INTRODUCTION

School is never out for the pro.
–Jim Williamson

Chances are you received this book as a gift from someone who believes in you. Someone who is counting on you. Someone who appreciates you and all that you do.

There, in three simple sentences, are the most meaningful compliments a salesperson can hope to hear. "I believe in you. I'm counting on you. I appreciate you." To earn this kind of praise from your sales manager or CEO is one thing, but to earn it from your customers is everything. It means that your customers trust you to make a significant difference in their business, their fortunes or their life. That, to me, is what our profession is all about. Practiced with high integrity, enthusiasm and care, professional sales is not merely about making a living for ourselves, it's about making a difference in the lives of those we serve.

That, too, is what this book is all about. Over the past 30 years I have met, observed or worked side-by-side with literally hundreds of high-performance salespeople. Among other things, I have learned that good people do not always make great salespeople, but great salespeople—those who stand the test of time—are always good people. I have learned that the great ones are life-long learners, that school is never out for the professionals, that they are constantly honing their knowledge, attitudes, skills and habits.

Here, then, are 24 stories comprising some of the simplest but most important lessons I've learned in a lifetime of sales and service. Some people still believe that professional sales is a full contact sport, the object of which is to use every trick in the book to run up the score on your client. If that's you, let me be the first to welcome you to a new and better reality. Enjoy this little book, and take it with you on your continuing journey to excellence. I believe in you. I'm counting on you. I appreciate you.

Jim Williamson

—Jim Williamson

COMPASS POINTS

If you don't know where you're going,
you might wind up someplace else.

—Yogi Berra

To ensure that you get the greatest possible value from this book, please take a few quiet minutes to complete the following reflective thinking exercise. A similar exercise is included at the end of the book.

1. My greatest strength in acquiring, developing and retaining customers:

_____

_____

2. One sales situation I'd like to handle better:

_____

_____

3. The person whose sales ability I most admire:

_____

4. The one quality (or qualities) I most admire about him or her:

_____

_____

5. If I get nothing else from this book, I'm going to keep an open mind and look for ways to improve the following:

_____

_____

A BOOK TO INSPIRE AND CELEBRATE YOUR ACHIEVEMENTS

PRIDE

*I, and millions like me, have educated
more people, created more jobs,
introduced more inventions, and have
given more laborers and business owners
a fuller life than anyone in history.*

—*Salesperson's Credo, 1928*

I found the 1928 sales creed above and saved it because it was true then, and it's still true today. The average American salesperson in today's economy keeps 33 men and women at work—33 people producing the product he or she sells—and is indirectly responsible for the livelihood of 130 people.

When you complete a sale, you have granted literally hundreds of people along the supply line one more unit of production, from the raw materials to the finished product. Our lives are better off because of salespeople. Look around at our technological advancements and all the comforts of living. Even the ideas for these had to be sold by someone. Someone had to be sold on manufacturing them, some on advertising them, some on marketing them and, yes, ultimately some on purchasing them.

Be proud of the repairman who noticed the bulge on the side of one of your tires and sold you a new set of radials. Or the travel agent who convinced you to close up shop and take your kids fishing in Alaska. Or the computer salesperson who sold you the new system that you thought you couldn't afford but which ultimately saved your business.

These salespeople, thousands of them, bring real value to our lives. I'm proud of them, I'm proud of you, and I'm proud to be one.

LESSONS LEARNED

- *The sales profession is far-reaching.*
- *Sales is the engine that drives our economy.*
- *Be proud to be in sales.*

INTEGRITY

To give real service, you must add something that cannot be bought or measured with money; and that is sincerity and integrity.

—*Donald A. Adams*

Here's something to think about. Every now and then I run across a sales organization that consistently out-sells its competitors—even though their product line and price are similar or identical.

Two different banks, for example, both offer the same product—loans. They are both conveniently located, and they both offer the same interest rates, the same terms, and the same collateral package. Why, then, does one bank consistently generate more loans than the other?

Why does one car dealership consistently out-sell another, even though both offer the same make and models, at about the same price, and in essentially the same marketplace? Same question for the real estate industry: Two realtors coexist side-by-side in the same neighborhood, and both draw most or many of their listings from the same multiple. Why, then, does one office consistently out-sell the other? I put this question to one of the most successful real estate brokers in the nation, and her answer is well worth considering:

"It's pretty simple, really. All other things being equal, we think people today want to know exactly who they're doing business with. People already know what kind of business we're in; what they really want to know is what kind of people we are.

"You can't fake it. Our offices are comprised of high-integrity, deeply experienced people who sincerely care about their customers, and who are actively involved in every community in which we serve. That's the truth. My job as CEO—and the job of our advertising people—is to simply tell the truth to as many people as we can. The rest takes care of itself."

LESSONS LEARNED:

- *Stand on principle.*
- *Know and live your values.*
- *Communicate your values to the customer.*

LISTEN

Wisdom is the reward you get for a lifetime of listening when you would have preferred to talk.

—*Doug Larson*

Imagine being a commissioned sales representative and making a billion-dollar sale. What an indescribable feeling! Now imagine that sale being abruptly cancelled just a few days later. That feeling, too, is indescribable.

Years ago I met a commercial airplane salesperson who was down in the dumps. This man had actually completed a billion-dollar fleet sale for his company, only to see it slip away in the eleventh hour. His CEO was shocked and placed a personal call to the President of the airlines in hopes of salvaging the sale.

"We thought this was a done deal," he pleaded. "May I ask why you changed your mind?"

"Your guy got complacent," replied the airline's President. "We specifically requested a different seating configuration. Your man failed to address that request, he didn't do his homework, he didn't listen—but your competitor heard us loud and clear."

Over the years I have learned again and again that listening is the master skill of all great sales professionals. A "master skill" is one that makes all other skills possible.

Believe it! It takes a great listener to be a great sales or service person. Active listening makes it easier to discover exactly what our customers want or need, rather than trying to convince them to buy what we are selling.

The billion-dollar principle is contained in these 12 simple words: We always learn more by asking and listening than telling and selling.

LESSONS LEARNED:

- *Listen actively to your customer.*
- *Don't just listen—hear!*
- *Don't just hear—follow through!*

TRUST

Like a hug from a child, trust is not something you demand, it's something you earn.

—Dan Zadra

One morning my good friend, Paul, tried and failed to buy a car at a nearby lot. The salesperson did a decent job, but when it came right down to making the purchase, Paul simply couldn't do it. Why? Because the salesperson was wearing sunglasses and kept saying, "Trust me."

That afternoon Paul went out of his way to buy the same car at the same price at a different lot across town. Now I hear you saying, "Geez, maybe your buddy shouldn't be so nit-picky. After all, sunglasses are good for the eyes, and 'trust me' is an everyday figure of speech." But the simple truth is that Paul really didn't want to purchase a $30,000 item from someone he didn't quite trust, or who wouldn't look him in the eye.

Believe me, Paul is not alone. Today, people everywhere want to know who they are buying from. That's one reason why so many companies are now prominently displaying their Corporate Values on the wall for all to see. Our values are the principles and standards we live by. They define how we expect to treat others; and they also set limits on our behavior.

Here is an actual Values Statement that I copied off the wall of a new car dealership just outside of Seattle:

—Trust—

We are honest, straightforward people. We care about our customers, our community and each other. We do not lie, cheat or stretch the truth. We are here to help our customers, not to sell them.

I would buy a car from a company like that in a heartbeat. In fact, I did.

LESSONS LEARNED

- *Trust takes time.*
- *You can collapse the time.*
- *Publishing your company values helps.*

GENUINE

Say what you mean.
Say exactly what you mean.
Say only what you mean.

—*Nido Qubien*

"I'll have your order in 8 days." (Two weeks later the order shows up).

"You can't find a lower price anywhere." (Unless, of course, you order directly from the factory).

"I'll personally manage your project, from start-up to completion. (Or someone in my department will if I'm busy).

It's up to each of us to put the image of the glib sales or service person to rest, once and for all. The motto for each of us should now become, "under-promise and over-deliver."

A survey of Fortune 500 buyers isolated 25 factors influencing the customer/salesperson relationship. Honest Communication was second only to Quality. Last on the list, believe it or not, was "Lowest Prices."

It's just this simple: If there's a problem with your client's order, say so.

If you need a 30-minute meeting, don't ask for 15.

If there's a way to save your client money, disclose it right away—even if it lowers your commission.

Always, and in every way, tell it like it is. Think before you announce how long something will take—and then deliver exactly what you promised, when promised, and for the amount promised.

LESSONS LEARNED:

- *Honesty is the first book of wisdom.*
- *Be sincere and straightforward.*
- *Under-promise and over-deliver.*

ATTITUDE

*If you honestly care about your
product, your service and your customer,
then show it. Lean into it!*

—Sam Walton, Wal–Mart

Attitude is an overworked word, but it's one that has special meaning for the top salespeople. Look up "attitude" in the dictionary and you'll see that it literally means "leaning." When it comes to professional sales and service, the truth is: we either lean toward or away from the customer—and our attitude always shows.

A Vice-President of sales for a large technology company once told me, "Jim, I will hire the person with the right attitude any day over the person with strong product knowledge and experience but possessing a poor attitude." I agree. Why? Because, as Wal-Mart's Sam Walton liked to say, "You can do everything right, but you'll still lose customers unless your attitude clearly says, 'You're important. I sincerely care about you. I'm here to do or find what's right for you. I'm ready to make life easier for you.'"

The key word is "sincerely." Our customers are smart people. They know the difference between someone who pretends to care and someone who really cares. So, if you're the one who really cares, take Sam's advice and distinguish yourself from all your competitors by "leaning into it."

Remember that a bad attitude isn't an affliction—you weren't born with it— and a good attitude isn't a gift from on high. Attitudes are actually habits of thought. They are choices that we make about how we will react to all areas of our life, including and especially our customers. You either habitually and sincerely care about your customers—and lean into it—or you don't. The choice is yours. Make it today.

LESSONS LEARNED:

- *Attitude is a choice and a habit.*
- *Lean into caring about your customer.*
- *When you care, people notice.*

RELATIONSHIPS

*Once you've formed a partnership with
your customer, you have just locked your competitors
out of the game.*

—*Larry Wilson*

My colleague, Larry Wilson, who co-authored "The One Minute Manager" with Ken Blanchard, maintains there are only three kinds of salespeople:

Phase 1 salespeople think of their clients as adversaries. To them, it appears that their clients stand between them and success. "Get them to sign the contract so we can take the money and run," is their official motto.

Phase 2 salespeople think of their clients as problems to be solved. Their square peg has to fit their client's square hole, or they have nothing to talk about. Because of that tight focus they tend to revert back to Phase 1 adversarial relationships whenever negotiations get rough.

Phase 3 salespeople focus on building long-term "trust relationships." In fact, they are so close to their clients, so flexible in understanding and anticipating their needs, that you might think they are actually on their clients' payroll. Guess which one of the three routinely has the highest income?

True story: A few years ago one of the top-3 computer software companies startled and re-energized their entire sales force by simply announcing a new type of bonus structure. "From now on," said the company's marketing director, "sales bonuses will not be based on the quantity of your short-term transactions—they will be based on the quality of your long-term relationships."

It was a gutsy move. Measuring "more" is easy, but measuring "better" is hard. Measuring better requires a trusting relationship and a long-term commitment to the customer's success, rather than a short-term commitment to the bottom line.

LESSONS LEARNED:

- *Focus on developing long-term trust relationships.*
- *Relationships first; transactions second.*
- *A good motto: My success is helping you achieve yours.*

LOVE AFFAIR

*When customers leave us for greener
pastures, they usually give price as the reason,
when in fact it's simple neglect.*

—John R. Graham

Could this be you? According to research by John R. Graham, customers feel we take them for granted; only show interest when we want an order; lavish our time on prospects; communicate mainly by invoice; are fixated only on big accounts; drop them like hot potatoes once we get them; don't follow through on promises; and satisfy our own bureaucracy rather than their needs.

Sure, you and I both know that you sincerely love your husband or wife or kids (or your customer), but what happens if you're too busy to show it?

The solution, of course, is to stop pressing for the order and start nurturing the relationship. Be a little more thoughtful, attentive and creative about the quality and frequency of your communication.

Regularly send valuable tips to your customers to help them prosper. Commemorate the anniversary of your first project together. Send occasional gifts that remind them of your mutual commitment to quality, service, teamwork, integrity, innovation, teamwork and loyalty.

Here's the principle: The great sales and service relationships really do resemble long-term love affairs. Love is nothing more than demonstrating massive liking. All other things being equal, your customers will naturally go (and stay) where they continuously feel massively and sincerely liked or loved.

LESSONS LEARNED:

- *If you care, show it.*
- *Stay in touch.*
- *Honor your customer, as you would your friend.*

PERSONAL NOTES

One handwritten note is worth
a thousand business letters.
—*Mark McCormack*

Rediscover the art of the personal note. Go out today and buy yourself a deluxe, soft-tip pen—one that fits naturally in your hand and writes with a satisfying flair. Then push your sophisticated PC aside and start writing some million-dollar personal notes to your customers.

What a welcome gift to your customer—a genuine handwritten card from you, tucked in a small invitation-sized envelope (something that is clearly not an invoice or a sales pitch) falling unexpectedly out of the jumble of your customer's morning mail. Will your note be noticed and read, first and foremost? Count on it.

By the way, a memo is not a note. You know the difference, we all do. Most memos come from the left side of the brain and are used to maintain distance between two parties. A good personal note comes straight from the heart and is meant to close the distance between two people by communicating candid feelings.

Yes, we're all busy, but one of the top mortgage bankers in Eastern Canada somehow finds time to faithfully send out 300 handwritten notes to his customers each month. He does it by allocating just one minute per note, and by writing just 15 notes per day.

So don't let a hectic schedule prevent you from expressing yourself in personal ways—that's what a note is all about. Your words need not be immortal. Just put a little of yourself in the envelope and send it off.

LESSONS LEARNED:

- *Nurture personal relationships with your customers.*
- *Make time to connect.*
- *Handwritten notes stand out from the clutter.*

OPEN UP

Openness breeds communication, and
communication holds the key to success.

—David Silverstein, Sun Microsystems

You know your product's features and benefits by heart and can't wait to convey them to your customers. But your customers can probably reveal five brilliant applications or benefits that you've never even thought of—if you will simply open up to them.

Motorola sales teams regularly invite their best customers to openly participate in their in-house sales training and product knowledge sessions. In effect, Motorola customers become Motorola salespeople for a day, brainstorming their product's features, benefits, and even the sales and marketing copy.

Sun Microsystems has a similar philosophy. "Our salespeople are good—they know our software systems inside and out," says former National Sales VP, Scott Johnson. "But clients like Amazon.com or the U.S. Air Force stretch the system and show us all kinds of new ways to apply and sell our own technology."

Dick Leard of Siemens, Inc. summed it up this way: "Open up to your customers and they'll show you the way. Our customers are partners in every sale. They supply the product specifications and even help us complete the administrative process."

Take a lesson from Dick Leard and explore new ways to partner with your customers. Ask yourself, "How can I be proactive and engage my customers in the entire sales process?"

LESSONS LEARNED:

- *Partner with your customers.*
- *Engage your customers in the sales process.*
- *Be open and receptive to new ideas.*

SMARTER

It is better to have the philosophy to out-think your competition than to out-spend them.

—Les Wolff

When you're in sales, it's always comforting to have a big advertising or promotional budget behind you. But when you're small, or when dollars are short, I always recommend piggybacking on your competitor's budget. I see this principle in action every day, but one of the best examples was provided by the innovative owner of a little hamburger stand deep in the Banff National Forest:

As you drive along a scenic stretch of the Canadian Highway, you notice a large sign that boldly proclaims, "The World's Greatest Hamburgers—100 Miles Ahead!" A little farther down the road is another sign: "Written Up in 50 Major Magazines—World's Greatest Hamburgers, 95 miles ahead!" These signs continue, in one form or another, and with obvious expense, every few miles for the entire 100-mile journey. By the time I finally arrived, everyone in our car was definitely ready for a burger. But, as you might expect, the parking lot of that hamburger stand was overflowing with people who had the same idea.

As I continued around the next bend, however—and this is the point—there stood a second hamburger stand. The only advertising expenditure of this particular establishment was a single sign that read: "World's Second Greatest Hamburgers!" It turns out that it, too,is perpetually crowded with the overflow from its famous competitor.

If you're Number 2, think like Avis. Ask yourself, "Which competitor is attracting prospects by out-spending me? Where is the overflow? How can I position myself at the same 'intersection' with those prospects?"

LESSONS LEARNED:

- *Know your competition.*
- *Try going "with" not "against" your competition.*
- *Let your lead competitors "draft" for you.*

SIZZLE

Don't just touch the head, touch the heart.
—Len Kallerson

If you check out amazon.com, you'll find several new and sophisticated books about the psychological factors involved in winning over the customer's mind. Or you can save yourself a few dollars by simply reading this classic excerpt from a 1940's Sears sales training manual. It was true then, and it's true today.

Please Don't Sell Me Things

- Don't sell me shoes; sell me style and comfort.

- Don't sell me candy; sell me happiness and the pleasure of good taste.

- Don't sell me furniture; sell me a home that has comfort, design and good taste.

- Don't sell me books; sell me pleasant hours and the profit of knowledge.

- Don't sell me toys; sell me playthings to make my children happy and keep them busy.

- Don't sell me tools; sell me the pleasure and profit of making fine things.

- Don't sell me refrigerators; sell me the convenience and better flavor of fresh foods.

- Don't sell me tires; sell me safety and low cost per mile.

- Don't sell me plows; sell me green fields of waving wheat.

- Please don't sell me things. Sell me ideas, benefits, visual pictures, feelings, self-respect, home life, happiness, and cost savings. Please, don't sell me things!

LESSONS LEARNED:

- *Sell benefits, not just features.*
- *Appeal to both emotion and logic.*
- *Ask yourself before every call, "What are the major benefits this person may be looking for?"*

TRACK RECORD

We judge ourselves by what we feel
capable of doing, while others judge us
by what we have already done.

—Bob Dolfay, Sunstrand Corp.

Salespeople are often told that yesterday is old news. "Put the past behind you—you're only as good as your next sale."

I disagree. What you or your company has done in the past—your track record—is pure gold, and often has everything to do with whether or not you make today's sale.

As far as I know, the military is the only organization that encourages their people to openly display their past accomplishments—their campaigns—on their chests where everyone can quickly and clearly see them. But there are several ways for you to accomplish the same result in sales.

Testimonials from previous clients are one way. Some say that testimonials are too corny to be effective, but they are extremely powerful when properly packaged and presented. For example, I am very proud of the excellent work my company has done with Boeing Aerospace, Xerox, Microsoft, AT&T and other excellent companies. The quality of this work was hard-earned. The letters of praise we've received from our clients, including the letter from AT&T acknowledging our assistance in helping them earn the Deming Award, distinguish us from newcomers in our field. We proudly display those letters in our corporate lobby and include copies (along with brief case histories of each project) in all our presentations.

Another method is to apply the principle of inference. For example, if TANG went to the moon with American astronauts, that infers that it must be a terrific breakfast drink. Disney University must be a sensational consulting firm if Fortune 500 companies seek their advice. If Crest is approved by the ADA.... if Japan buys more Fords than any other U.S. car...if Michael Jordan wears Nikes...if Wilfred Brimley eats Quaker Oats...then it must be the right thing to do!

Today, imagine three new ways to harness the power of testimonials, case histories or inference in your work with clients.

LESSONS LEARNED:

- *Ask satisfied customers to write their positive comments in letter format.*
- *Document and model your business sucesses.*
- *Display and share your successes with others.*

PARTNERS

All around you are
potential marketing partners…
if you will only stop and look.

—*Dennis Brandon, Westmark Hotels*

Let's talk about referrals for a second. I know, I know. . .building a steady referral base is Basic Sales Training, 101. You probably already have that under control, but I doubt it.

I doubt it because most salespeople are primarily focused on either serving their customers or fighting their competition. Forget your competition for a moment, forget your enemies. Focus instead on developing more friends, turning more people who already know and like you into passionate advocates for your products and services.

Today, ask yourself, "What are two or three obvious new possibilities for cross-marketing, partnering or reciprocal referrals?" At the end of the year a photography studio sends a free 5 x 7 photo from the year's previous shoots as a Holiday gift to every customer—and then asks them to refer a friend.

Nordstrom stores "partner" with the very best nearby hotels in each city in a reciprocal referral program: "You guide out-of-town visitors to Nordstrom, and we'll guide them to your hotel."

Hyatt Hotels "partner" with 35,000 travel agents and event planners. And dozens of companies of all sizes partner with Amway's one million independent distributors.

Carlos Ramirez once said, "What a world this would be if we just built bridges instead of walls." I agree. Instead of trying to wall off your competitors, try building more bridges to your friends.

LESSONS LEARNED:

- *Nurture your referral system on a daily basis.*
- *Practice the principle of "give and get." Determine what you can give to get more referrals.*
- *Focus more on your friends and acquaintances, less on your competition.*

STAY CLOSE

*It's a good idea to sample
your own wares once in awhile.*

—Dunc Muncy

Sales and service people are often reminded to "hold the product high." In our seminars, however, we also advise people to "knock their own product or service off the pedestal once in awhile." There's no better way to do this than to put yourself in the customer's shoes—and then look for problems.

McDonald's managers anonymously eat lunch at each other's restaurants, and then report on the total experience. Hilton employees check in to each other's hotels, dressed as tourists. Chrysler managers still take their turns at the service desk. PepsiCo's corporate officers still make regular sales calls.

The same principle can and should be applied to everyone in your company. The truth is, most frontline employees do not have the slightest idea what actually happens to their product or service, once it leaves the salesperson's hands. Suppose you videotaped customer interviews for employees; or invited customers in to speak to employees; or arranged for employees to visit your customers' companies; or at least ran regular customer profiles in your company newsletter? Wouldn't everyone in your company feel closer to your sales team and your customers?

Wouldn't every employee, from the bottom to the top, have the satisfaction of seeing and feeling the end results of your sale? Wouldn't you be a tighter team?

LESSONS LEARNED:

- *View your business through your customer's eyes.*
- *Try to experience what your customer may experience.*
- *Identify problems or challenges and fix them.*

CONSTANCY

It's not what you do now and then,
it's what you do every time that counts.

—*Mary Augustine*

An unusual word, "constancy." Amazon.com lists thousands of books for salespeople, and I doubt any contain the word "constancy," but they should. In my book, constancy is the holy grail of high performance sales and service. Constancy is the quality that builds long-term trust between you and your clients; and long-term trust is the gateway to recurring sales and repeat business.

Constancy comes from the Latin, *com*, which means "together" and *stare*, which means "to stand." There you have it. The golden key to those cherished long-term trust relationships is, quite simply, to "stand together" with your customers. And not just once in awhile, but every single solitary time.

In all my years in sales I have never heard a client say, "Jim, the thing I treasure about our relationship is that I can 'almost always' count on you to be there for me." Almost always does not build trust, it subverts it. Almost always is not nearly good enough for your client, or for you, or for me.

Constancy means that you stand with your client through thick and thin—even battling your own company's bureaucracy if necessary—and that you trust each other again and again.

Constancy is different from consistency. Consistency means your client can rely on you to do or deliver the same thing over and over. Constancy means that your client can trust you to do the best thing for his or her particular and ever-changing circumstances, whatever it takes.

LESSONS LEARNED:

- *Align with your customer.*
- *Fight for your customer.*
- *Trust is built through constancy.*

PERSISTENCE

When nothing seems to help, I go and look at a stonecutter hammering away at his rock, perhaps a hundred times without as much as a crack showing in it. Yet, at the hundred and first blow it will split in two, and I know it was not that blow that did it—but all that had gone before.

—*Jacob Riis*

The stonecutter verse by Jacob Riis has always been a favorite of mine, and I have shared it with many people in our seminars. My grandfather, who was born in Norway, was a proud "stenhugger" (Norwegian for stonecutter). He eventually emigrated to America where he practiced his trade. Watching him as a young child taught me one of my earliest lessons about persistence.

Another Norwegian, Larry Sund, has risen over the past thirty years to become one of the top salespeople for Patterson Dental Corporation, but I think he has some stonecutter in his blood.

"Let me tell you, Jim, it wasn't easy in the beginning," said Larry. "In my first few years with Patterson they assured us that if we took good care of the customer, developed a relationship of trust, and kept their best interests in mind, the sales would follow."

He went on to recount, "In my very first year there was a dentist in my territory who I dearly wanted to become a customer. I called on him month after month with no apparent progress. What made matters worse was how rudely he treated me. This made me even more determined to win him over."

Finally, in the seventh month, the dentist said, "Larry, come in and look at my new operating room. I want you to go ahead and develop a list of Patterson equipment that you believe should go in there."

"What would you like to see in here?" I stammered.

"Larry, I'm leaving that up to you." And Patterson equipped it with their latest technology at the time.

By the way, persistence sometimes works both ways. The best part about Larry's story is that it has no ending. Thirty years later, that dentist was still a loyal Patterson Dental customer.

LESSONS LEARNED:

- *Qualify your opportunities.*
- *Treat resistance with persistence.*
- *Know the difference between "pest" and persistence.*

TRADE MINDS

What a wonderful miracle if only we could look through each other's eyes for an instant.
—Henry David Thoreau

Smith & Hawken, one of our nation's most accomplished direct marketing companies, invented the annual Go for Broke report. It is an attempt by every person in the company to list everything in his/her department (or anywhere else at Smith & Hawken) that he or she believes is broken or needs fixing— including relationships.

"I haven't seen or heard of anything that improves a company's sales and service so thoroughly as the Go For Broke," said Hawken—so the practice was continued.

Most of the things needing repair were subsequently fixed by the person identifying the problem. But in many cases, the problems were the direct result of many years of poor communication between the sales and service departments. They were both serving the same customer, and they thought they were communicating with each other, but they really weren't. Both departments were lost in their own little worlds.

Fixing these problems required a new level of teamwork and conversation between sales and service, so Hawken gave the same advice to his world-class staff as I am giving you here:

If you're in sales, take a service person to lunch. If you're in service, take a salesperson to lunch. If you're in accounting, take them both to lunch. Trade minds with each other. See the world through each other's eyes—and then come up with fresh new solutions that will WOW your customers.

LESSONS LEARNED:

- *Identify your business' weaknesses.*
- *Communicate and interact with other departments to identify issues.*
- *Trade ideas for discovering fresh solutions.*

RESULTS

There are no gold medals for the 95-yard dash.
—Max DePree, Herman Miller Company

It was Rudyard Kipling who said, "We have forty million reasons for failure, but not a single excuse." Maybe Kipling was in sales.

Somewhere in my travels, a wise old sales manager passed on to me his "Alibi Chart for Salespeople" and I have included it here. My advice to all professional sales and service people is to hang it prominently on the wall as a daily reminder of what you don't want to hear in your hallowed halls.

Who wants to hear, "We almost made the sale. We almost met our delivery date. We almost met our sales projections."

Instead, let the world hear us say, "We did!"

Alibi Chart For Salespeople

January. Need time to recover from the holidays.

February. My best clients have gone South for winter vacation.

March. Everybody's worrying about income tax.

April. Spent too much money first quarter.

May. Revising annual budgets; concerned about next six months.

June. Starting to plan for summer vacation.

July. Everybody away on vacation.

August. Everybody still away.

September. Everybody back; need time to catch up.

October. Waiting to see how 4th quarter budget comes out.

November. Everybody too upset over elections.

December. Clients too busy with the Holidays.

LESSONS LEARNED:

- *Focus on what you want, not what you don't want.*
- *Focus on why you can, not why you can't.*
- *Accept accountability; no excuses.*

TIME

Lost, somewhere between sunrise
and sunset: 60 golden minutes, each set
with 60 diamond seconds. No reward
is offered, for they are lost forever.

—Unknown

Time is one of a salesperson's most precious possessions. Each of us gets the same amount every day—it's the only fair thing—but there's a huge difference in how we each choose to use it.

I frequently hear salespeople talk about "saving" time, but that's a fallacy. The truth is, we can't save time, we can only spend it. Starting today, spend it wisely.

Of the "Top-50" time-wasters, here are the 12 that can be corrected easiest and fastest:

- Surfing the web.
- Not doing first things first.
- Pet projects or outside activities.
- Random yacking or schmoozing.
- Cluttered desk or office.

- Poor filing system.
- Poor expense reporting system.
- Inefficient proposal system.
- Inability to say "no."
- E-mail-itis.
- Meeting-itis.
- Rambling phone conversations.

Today, do yourself and your company a giant favor. Choose three of the above and make a plan to permanently eliminate them from your day. At the same time, recommit to writing your daily "To Do" list, focusing first on the top five, doing first things first, and one thing at a time.

LESSONS LEARNED:

- *Write a daily "to do" list.*
- *Do first things first, and one thing at a time.*
- *Ask yourself on a constant basis, "Is this the best use of my time right now?"*

AGES & STAGES

To find out what makes a person tick, don't ask their age. Ask instead about their goals and aspirations.
—*Faith Popcorn*

It's common practice for sales and marketing people to profile their market—but beware of "ageism."

Whether they are 18 or 80, people today defy the previous stereotypes. Flynn Sharpe of Vital Data Group advises salespeople and marketers to abandon age as an accurate indicator of buying decisions. "Stop thinking about ages and think instead about stages of life," says Sharpe. For example, today's grandmother may look and think more like model Cheryl Tieggs than the venerable granny of thirty years ago. At 60, she may just be hitting her stride as a CEO, or returning to college for her MBA degree.

I ran smack into ageism the year I subscribed to AARP Magazine. AARP is a terrific organization, and they offer spectacular services for people over 50. But once I landed on their list, I was bombarded by mailers from companies that specialize in marketing to people like me who are supposedly entering our

"Golden Years." Bull! Virtually nothing in those mailers made sense to me or my friends—and I've heard the same complaints from people in their twenties and thirties who are offended by the Gen-X marketing stereotypes.

The next time you're preparing a sales presentation, remember this: At 16, Shane Gould won five Olympic medals; at 16, Mozart wrote his first symphony; at 23, Stephen Jobs founded Apple; at 52, Ray Kroc opened his first McDonald's; and at 78, Grandma Moses started painting.

Sales, too, is a profession where people often excel way past the traditional retirement age. I know of a car salesman in Seattle who, at age 102, had outlived his regular customers, but was still serving their children and grandchildren.

"Stages not ages" means that it's what people do, not when they're supposed to do it, that really counts.

LESSONS LEARNED:

- *Avoid stereotypes.*
- *Treat everyone as an individual.*
- *Age is not important unless you're a cheese.*

TENACITY

Never, never, never quit.
—Winston Churchill

For 30 years I have known, taught or worked with hundreds of high-profile salespeople—the best of the best in their respective industries. These perennial top performers are all different from each other in many ways, but they share one common trait—tenacity!

Sales is no place for pansies. This is especially true for the road warriors among us. How many times have I sat down for dinner at some airport hotel and heard a conversation like this at the next table: "My wallet got stolen in Newark. The plane was snowbound in Detroit. My rental car broke down in Mobile, Alabama. By the time I got to the hotel, I had missed the 6:00 PM check-in and they had given my room away. But I'm here, now, and I'm ready to present."

It would be nice to report that all these horror stories end on a happy note, that the sale is always made in the end, and that our hero comes home with the contract. But you and I both know that's not always the case. What I can report is that, in the long run, the top performers are the ones who, as good old Winston Churchill said, "never, never, never quit."

Top performers are goal-directed and committed. Their focus on the long-range picture helps them deal more comfortably with short-term frustrations. They stay in touch with their commitment, realizing that anybody can start something, but it takes a person of character to finish.

Top performers are resilient. They treat all setbacks as temporary. They know that the tide goes out now and then, but they also know that it always comes back in.

Finally, the top performers are resourceful. When faced with an obstacle, they believe there's always a way—over, under, around or through—and they find it. You never hear a top performer say, "Gee, can we really pull this off?" Instead, you hear them say, "*How* can we pull this off?"

LESSONS LEARNED:

- *Be solution oriented, always find a way.*
- *Commit to your goals and long-term picture.*
- *Treat all setbacks as temporary.*

THANK YOU

No matter what we do, somebody helps us.

—*Wilma Rudolph*

Sometimes we think we do it all ourselves. But for every successful sales presentation we make, a hundred invisible hands support us at every turn.

A sales rep flew into Chicago late one night and checked into the Airport Marriott. At 9:00 sharp the next morning she had a presentation across town that could make or break her company. It was still dark when she awoke, but an eerie light shimmered through her fifth floor window. Quickly, she flung open the curtains and her heart sank. Every hotel and car on the strip was buried under a foot of new snow. No way could she drive through this muck to her appointment.

But wait. As her eyes adjusted, she noticed the distant freeways had already been cleared by the City. From there, she gazed straight down at her own parking lot and finally realized that hers was the only hotel on the strip that was clear of snow. While she had slept, someone from the Marriott had broomed the snow off every car and shoveled a clear path out of the lot!

Did she make her presentation? Yes, but that's not the point of the story. The real point is that she sat down as soon as she got home and fired off two thoughtful letters of appreciation—one to the City of Chicago and one to the Marriott.

In our business, no one ever does anything of real consequence entirely on their own—we all have someone to thank for our accomplishments. Today make your list and let them know how you feel.

LESSONS LEARNED:

- *Everyone appreciates being appreciated.*
- *Every day find a way to do something nice for someone.*
- *If you're too busy to help others, you're too busy.*

DREAMS

Follow your dreams, they know the way.
—*Kobi Yamada*

Most salespeople are born optimists. They are not just dreamers, they are doers. Pound for pound, salespeople are probably the most goal-oriented people in any profession. We have to be! Tackling our company's revenue projections; getting paid on performance; staying perpetually motivated; weathering setbacks and rejection—these all require expert goal-setting skills and discipline. And one more thing: Dreams.

In our sales workshops, there's a key spot where we stop to remind ourselves about the fundamental power of converting our dreams into goals, and our goals into plans. Every salesperson knows this stuff by heart, but sometimes we lose touch, so I like to end with this little story from Les Brown:

An elderly man, in the final days of his life, is lying in bed alone. He awakens to see a large group of people clustered around his bed. Their faces are loving but sad. Confused, the old man smiles weakly and whispers, "You must be my childhood friends, come to say good-bye. I am so grateful."

Moving closer, the tallest figure gently grasps the old man's hand and replies, "Yes, we are your best and oldest friends, but long ago you abandoned us. For we are the unfulfilled dreams of your youth. We are the unrealized hopes that you once felt deeply in your heart, but never pursued. We are the unique talents that you never refined, the special gifts you never discovered. Old friend, we have not come to comfort you, but to die with you."

My closing message is always the same: Let's live each day so we'll have no regrets at the end. Follow your dreams, they know the way.

LESSONS LEARNED:

- *Stay in touch with your dreams.*
- *Turn your dreams into goals.*
- *Convert your goals into action plans.*

COMPASS POINTS

We can do more than work, we can grow.
—Suzanne Hoonan

1. The 5 most important ideas I gained from this book:

_____

_____

_____

2. Specific techniques, ideas, skills or strategies I will develop and put into practice:

_____

_____

_____

3. If I do nothing else but apply the value received from one lesson, that lesson is:

_____

_____

_____

A SALE IS NOT SOMETHING YOU PURSUE. IT'S WHAT HAPPENS TO YOU WHILE YOU ARE IMMERSED IN SERVING YOUR CUSTOMER.

—JIM WILLIAMSON

ABOUT ADVANTAGE LEARNING SERVICES

ALS is a Seattle based training and consulting firm formed to assist companies and their employees in achieving greater levels of performance and effectiveness.

Over the past 20 years ALS has developed and continues to offer seminars in the following areas:
• Leadership • Team Development • Attitude Development • Sales Management • Change Management • Sales • Service
• Presentation • Negotiation

ALS has a national account base, many of which participate in their certified train-the-trainer programs. The following is a partial list of our clients:

AT&T	Coca–Cola USA	Weyerhaeuser
Micron	Qwest	I.B.M.
Bank of America	Discover Card	Xerox
Microsoft	U.S. Bank	Lucent
Boeing	Hospital Corp. of	
Nike	America	

Other published products offered by Advantage Learning Services:

"Lessons Learned" Personal Library Series:
I. Sales. II. Service. III. Presentation. IV. Negotiation

Audio/CD/Video/DVD Programs:
• *Increasing Human Effectiveness* • *Team Development*
• *Assessments and Cultural Audits*

LOOKING FOR A KEYNOTE SPEAKER?

Would you like to make these books and other high interest topics come alive at your next sale or service meeting?

ALS provides a number of high interest Keynote Presentations in live multi-media format that will keep your audience's attention, assisting in your meeting's success. Four very popular keynote presentations at this time are:

- *Characteristics of High Performance Salespeople*
- *Gut–Level Leadership*
- *Managing Change in a Competitive Marketplace*
- *Maintaining Winning Attitudes In Turbulent Times*

To discuss availability, contact us at:

Advantage Learning Services
6947 Coal Creek Parkway, Suite 2600
Newcastle, WA 98059-3136

Phone: 425-747-4484
E-mail: advlerarn@worldnet.att.net

Visit us online today and experience our instant Culture Audit at www.advlearnsys.com

ABOUT THE AUTHOR

Photo Christine Scholz

Jim Williamson is co-founder and CEO of Advantage Learning Services, a private consulting and training organization based in Seattle, Washington.

Prior to founding ALS, Jim served as Sr. Vice-President of Sales & Marketing for Edge Learning Institute, currently an alliance business partner. He also served as District Sales Manager and, later, Director of Marketing for Prentice Hall's Educational Book Division in Englewood Cliffs, New Jersey. Earlier in his professional career he worked as a psychology teacher/guidance counselor at a high school, community college and Washington State prison.

Currently he specializes in the area of helping to develop High Performance Sales & Service Cultures within organizations. He has designed, written and published a number of customized sales and service programs which have been distributed to thousands of employees over the past 20 years.

Do you have a favorite story you'd like to submit? We would like to hear and consider your "lessons learned" for a future edition. Please submit to: advlearn@worldnet.att.net.